D1035097

X
975.7   The Colony of South
JEF   Carolina   AME
4/2016

ST. MARY PARISH LIBRARY
FRANKLIN, LOUISIANA

Spotlight on the 13 Colonies
Birth of a Nation

★ ★ ★ ★ ★ ★ ★ ★ ★ ★ ★ ★

THE COLONY OF
SOUTH
CAROLINA

Joyce Jeffries

PowerKiDS
press™

NEW YORK

Published in 2016 by The Rosen Publishing Group, Inc.
29 East 21st Street, New York, NY 10010

Copyright © 2016 by The Rosen Publishing Group, Inc.

All rights reserved. No part of this book may be reproduced in any form without permission
in writing from the publisher, except by a reviewer.

Editor: Katie Kawa
Book Design: Andrea Davison-Bartolotta

Photo Credits: Cover, pp. 10, 17 North Wind Picture Archives; p. 4 Science & Society Picture Library/
Getty Images; p. 5 MPI/Stringer/Getty Images; p. 6 Magicpiano/Wikimedia Commons; p. 7 iofoto/
Shutterstock.com; p. 8 Chiyacat/Shutterstock.com; p. 9 (main) Phill Doherty/Shutterstock.com; p. 9 (inset)
Henrik Larsson/Shutterstock.com; p. 11 American Spirit/Shutterstock.com; pp. 12–13 (bottom) Everett Historical/
Shutterstock.com; p. 13 (top) Franz Xaver/Wikimedia Commons; pp. 14–15 Kean Collection/Getty Images;
p. 19 (main) Harpischord246/Wikimedia Commons; p. 19 (inset) Hulton Archive/Stringer/Getty Images; p. 21
SuperStock/Getty Images; p. 22 VectorPic/Shutterstock.com.

Jeffries, Joyce.
The colony of South Carolina / by Joyce Jeffries.
p. cm. — (Spotlight on the 13 colonies: Birth of a nation)
Includes index.
ISBN 978-1-4994-0582-8 (pbk.)
ISBN 978-1-4994-0583-5 (6 pack)
ISBN 978-1-4994-0585-9 (library binding)
1. South Carolina — History — Colonial period, ca. 1600 - 1775 — Juvenile literature. 2. South Carolina —
History — 1775 - 1865 — Juvenile literature. I. Jeffries, Joyce. II. Title.
F272.J44 2015
975.7/02—d23

Manufactured in the United States of America

CPSIA Compliance Information: Batch #WS15PK: For further information contact Rosen Publishing, New York, New York at 1-800-237-9932.

Contents

Explorers in South Carolina

Long before European explorers came to North America, Native Americans called this continent home. **Ancestors** of Native Americans came to what is now South Carolina at least 12,000 years ago, and some believe they may have been there over 40,000 years ago! Native American tribes that lived in present-day South Carolina included the Cherokee, Yamasee, and Catawba.

Europeans began to arrive in South Carolina in the 1500s. Francisco Gordillo of Spain became the first European to see the South Carolina coast in 1521. Five years later, Lucas Vásquez de Ayllón tried to establish a colony in South Carolina, but it failed. Another unsuccessful attempt to colonize this area came in 1562, when Frenchman Jean Ribault and a group of settlers landed on Parris Island, off the coast of South Carolina. The next year, those settlers returned to France. However, the Spanish landed on Parris Island in 1566. They created their own military base there, called Santa Elena, which lasted until 1587.

Native Americans attacking Ayllón's settlers

Prom. Lupi.

This map from the late 1500s shows what it may have looked like when Jean Ribault's ships sailed up the Port Royal River to explore South Carolina.

A Permanent Colony

South Carolina didn't become a **permanent** colony until the 1600s. In 1629, Charles I, king of England, gave Robert Heath land in North America to establish a colony. Heath named his land Carolina in honor of the king, whose name in Latin is Carolus. However, he wasn't able to establish a permanent colony there.

In 1663, King Charles II gave Carolina to eight men through a **charter** that set up a proprietary colony. This kind of colony is one that's privately owned. The colony of Carolina included the areas that would become known as North Carolina and South Carolina.

The first permanent settlement in Carolina was founded in 1670 by William Sayle. Located on the banks of the Ashley River and called Charles Town, the settlement was the capital of the Carolina colony. Sayle was Charles Town's first governor. Within 10 years, the settlement had grown and moved to its current location on the **peninsula** formed by the Ashley and the Cooper Rivers.

map of Charles Town, 1733

Charles Town, which is now called Charleston, is still a popular city to visit in South Carolina because of its rich history.

Life in the Colony

As settlers began to arrive in Carolina after 1670, they had to learn to live in a world very different from the places they came from. The first settlers in the area that would become South Carolina tried to grow a number of crops for food and for trading. Some crops, such as corn, were successful and helped colonists survive. Others, such as **sugarcane**, failed.

Some settlers in this colony couldn't tend to their farms because they became sick. Malaria is a **disease** that killed settlers in Carolina. It's passed on by mosquitoes and causes people to have a very high fever.

The early settlers in Carolina made money by trading with the Native Americans who lived in the area. The Cherokee and Catawba traded animal furs and skins for guns and tools from the settlers. Then, the settlers sold the furs to people in England. Deerskins were the most common skins sold by settlers in the southern part of Carolina.

deerskin

Mosquitoes are common in warm, wet areas of land, which are found throughout South Carolina, especially in the Low Country area along the coast. That's why so many settlers in the Carolina colony became sick with malaria.

Difficult Times

Farming in the southern part of Carolina grew when rice was introduced as a major crop. Rice farming was so successful that it allowed farmers to create plantations, or very large farms, that often relied on slaves brought to the colony from Africa. Slavery became an important part of the economy in Carolina. Thousands of men, women, and children worked on plantations as slaves.

Although Carolina's economy was strong, life wasn't always easy in this colony. Fighting broke out between colonists and Native Americans. In 1715, a war began between settlers and members of the Yamasee tribe.

Pirates were also a danger to this colony. Charleston was a very important port city, so pirates would attack ships as they entered or left. Two of the most famous pirates to attack Carolinian ships were Blackbeard and Stede Bonnet. William Rhett, a colonial **militia** leader from Charleston, captured Bonnet in 1718. The pirate was later hanged for his crimes.

Charleston Harbor

Plantations in what is now South Carolina often had large homes where the owners lived. People can still visit many of these homes today.

Drayton Hall on the Ashley River

Slavery in South Carolina

In 1729, Carolina was officially separated into two colonies: North Carolina and South Carolina. King George I of Britain then made South Carolina a royal colony. This meant it would be ruled by the king. Robert Johnson became the governor of this new royal colony.

Ten years later, the Stono Rebellion occurred near the Stono River in South Carolina. On September 9, 1739, 20 slaves stole guns and used them to start an uprising, gaining more followers throughout the day. During this slave rebellion, between 20 and 25 white colonists were killed before the slaves were captured. They were later hanged, and **strict** new laws were passed to control the slaves in the colony.

Slaves often lived in poor conditions in separate quarters, or living areas, on plantations. When indigo was introduced as another major crop in South Carolina, more slaves were needed to keep up with the demand for it.

Slaves were needed more than ever in South Carolina as indigo, which was grown in the colony, became more popular in Europe. This crop was used to make blue dye, and it could be sold to Britain and many other countries. Rice and indigo were South Carolina's two major crops during the colonial period.

indigo

The Cost of War

By the middle of the 1700s, there was growing unrest in the colonies. The British and their Native American **allies** fought the French and their Native American allies in the French and Indian War (1754–1763). To help pay for the war, Britain decided to tax the colonies. These taxes would also pay for keeping British soldiers in the colonies to keep peace between the colonists and Native Americans.

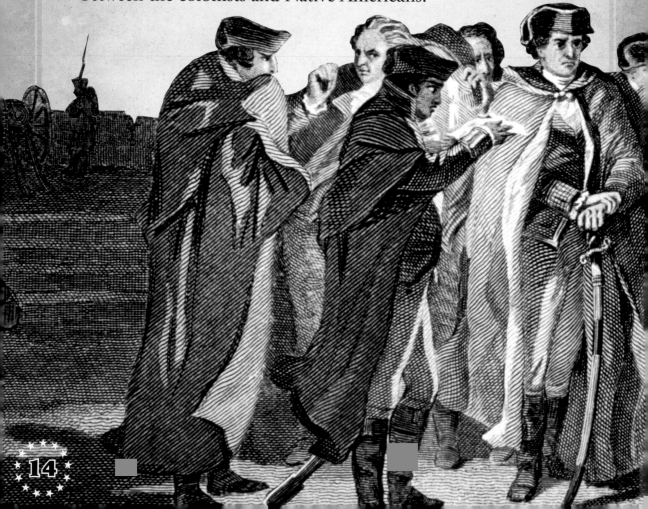

In 1765, Britain passed the Stamp Act, which taxed nearly all paper goods in the colonies. Christopher Gadsden of South Carolina became one of the most outspoken **opponents** of the Stamp Act. He represented South Carolina at the Stamp Act Congress. This meeting of colonial leaders took place in New York City in 1765. Gadsden and others spoke out against what they felt were unfair taxes. They wanted to **petition** the king and the leaders of Parliament, which is the British lawmaking body, to make these taxes fairer for the colonists.

The French and Indian War was part of a larger worldwide war that was known in Europe as the Seven Years' War.

Fighting Unfair Taxes

Parliament repealed, or did away with, the Stamp Act in 1766. However, Britain then created new taxes. In order to get around paying taxes, colonists sometimes boycotted, or refused to buy, British goods.

On December 16, 1773, patriots in Boston, Massachusetts, dumped a load of tea into Boston Harbor to protest the taxation of tea by the British. These patriots felt it wasn't fair for colonists to be taxed by the British without equal representation in Parliament. Colonists in South Carolina showed their support for their fellow colonists in Boston by removing tea from ships in Charleston's harbor and locking it up.

Representatives from the colonies met in Philadelphia, Pennsylvania, in September 1774. This gathering became known as the First Continental Congress, and it was held to fight what they felt were Britain's unfair taxes and laws. Gadsden was one of South Carolina's representatives at the First Continental Congress. The others were John Rutledge, Edward Rutledge, Thomas Lynch Jr., and Henry Middleton.

This illustration shows a Carolina woman chasing a tax collector off her property.

Revolution!

The growing **tension** between the British and the colonists eventually led to war. On April 19, 1775, battles were fought at Lexington and Concord in Massachusetts, and the American Revolution began. All 13 colonies, including South Carolina, raised troops to help fight the British.

Colonial leaders met again in May 1775. This Second Continental Congress organized the Continental army and named George Washington its leader. The representatives also voted on whether or not the colonies should be independent of British rule. At first, the representatives from South Carolina—along with those from New York, New Jersey, Pennsylvania, Delaware, and Maryland—didn't vote in favor of independence. However, they eventually came to support the idea of the colonies forming their own nation.

The Declaration of Independence was written to proclaim the colonies' independence and explain why they were breaking away from Britain. On July 4, 1776, it was accepted by the representatives. Four South Carolinians signed the Declaration of Independence: Edward Rutledge, Arthur Middleton, Thomas Heyward Jr., and Thomas Lynch Jr.

Edward Rutledge

Edward Rutledge can be seen standing on the far right in this painting of the signing of the Declaration of Independence.

Battles in South Carolina

South Carolina was the site of some of the most important battles of the American Revolution. Over 200 battles were fought there. South Carolinians—including Francis Marion, Thomas Sumter, and Andrew Pickens—became important military leaders in the war.

As the American Revolution in the North turned in favor of the patriots, the British sent more troops to the South, including South Carolina. They believed they had more supporters, known as loyalists, in those states. For a time, the British had control over important areas of the South, including Charleston.

Near the end of the war, two battles were fought in South Carolina that led to the **defeat** of the British. The Battle of Kings Mountain, which took place on October 7, 1780, is known as one of the turning points in the war. The Battle of Cowpens was another turning point. It led to the American victory over the weakened British troops at Yorktown, Virginia, in October 1781. The British **surrendered** after their loss at Yorktown.

The Battle of Cowpens occurred on January 17, 1781. The fighting lasted less than an hour, and when it was over, the Americans were one big step closer to winning the war.

A New State

In 1783, the Treaty of Paris was signed, and the American Revolution officially ended. The next step on the road to independence was to create a lasting government for the states. The states were originally governed by the Second Continental Congress. Henry Middleton and Henry Laurens from South Carolina each served as president of the Congress for a time.

The Articles of Confederation were **ratified** on March 1, 1781, and they set up a government that gave much more power to the states than to the national government. This didn't work very well, so a convention was called in 1787 to try to improve the Articles of Confederation. Charles Pinckney, Charles Cotesworth Pinckney, John Rutledge, and Pierce Butler represented South Carolina at the convention. In the end, the convention wrote a new Constitution and became known as the Constitutional Convention. South Carolina ratified the Constitution on May 23, 1788, becoming the eighth state to officially join the United States.

Glossary

ally: A group that helps another group in a war.

ancestor: One of the people from whom a person is descended.

charter: A document issued by a government that gives rights to a person or group.

defeat: Loss.

disease: A sickness.

militia: A group of people who are not an official part of the armed forces of a country but are trained like soldiers.

opponent: A person who is against something.

peninsula: A piece of land that is almost completely surrounded by water and attached to a larger land area.

permanent: Lasting for a long time or forever.

petition: To ask for something in a formal way.

ratify: To formally approve.

strict: Severe.

sugarcane: A tall grass that is grown in warm places and is a source of sugar.

surrender: To agree to stop fighting because you know you will not win or succeed.

tension: A state in which two people, groups, or countries disagree with and feel anger toward each other.

Index

Primary Source List

p. 5 *Port Royal, Carolina.* Created by Jacques Le Moyne de Morgues and engraved by Theodor de Bry. Engraving. 1591. Included in *A brief narration of those things which befell the French in the province of Florida in America*. Published in Frankfurt, Germany, 1591.

p. 6 Map of Charles Town, South Carolina. Created by William Henry Toms and R.W. Seale. Engraving on paper. 1733. Inset from a larger map of North America, titled *A map of the British Empire in America with the French and Spanish settlements adjacent thereto*, by Henry Popple. Now kept in the Library of Congress Geography and Maps Division, Washington, D.C.

p. 11 Drayton Hall. Designed by John Drayton. Brick. ca. 1740. Now located at 3380 Ashley River Road, Charleston, South Carolina.

Websites

Due to the changing nature of Internet links, PowerKids Press has developed an online list of websites related to the subject of this book. This site is updated regularly. Please use this link to access the list: www.powerkidslinks.com/s13c/sc